55 Italian Recipes for Home

By: Kelly Johnson

Table of Contents

- Spaghetti Bolognese
- Margherita Pizza
- Risotto alla Milanese
- Tiramisu
- Fettuccine Alfredo
- Osso Buco
- Caprese Salad
- Eggplant Parmesan
- Minestrone Soup
- Ravioli with Tomato Sauce
- Gnocchi
- Pasta Carbonara
- Cannoli
- Pesto Genovese
- Lasagna
- Bruschetta
- Veal Saltimbocca
- Cioppino
- Amatriciana Sauce
- Polenta
- Arancini
- Panzanella
- Orecchiette with Broccoli Rabe
- Tiramisu
- Risotto ai Funghi
- Panna Cotta
- Shrimp Scampi
- Prosciutto and Melon
- Pasta Puttanesca
- Zuppa Toscana
- Cacio e Pepe
- Pistachio Gelato
- Salted Cod (Baccalà)
- Veal Marsala
- Pappardelle with Wild Boar Ragu

- Cannelloni
- Calzone
- Zabaione
- Eggplant Caponata
- Pasta Primavera
- Saffron Risotto
- Porchetta
- Grilled Calamari
- Lemon Sorbet
- Bagna Cauda
- Pecorino Cheese with Honey
- Sausage and Peppers
- Farfalle with Salmon Cream Sauce
- Neapolitan Pizza
- Stracciatella Soup
- Grilled Branzino
- Anchovy and Garlic Butter Crostini
- Beef Carpaccio
- Spinach and Ricotta Stuffed Shells
- Limoncello Sorbet

Spaghetti Bolognese

Ingredients:

- 1 lb ground beef
- 1 onion, finely chopped
- 2 cloves garlic, minced
- 1 carrot, grated
- 1 celery stalk, finely chopped
- 1 can (28 oz) crushed tomatoes
- 2 tablespoons tomato paste
- 1 cup beef broth
- 1/2 cup red wine (optional)
- 1 teaspoon dried oregano
- 1 teaspoon dried basil
- Salt and pepper to taste
- 2 tablespoons olive oil
- 1 lb spaghetti
- Grated Parmesan cheese for serving

Instructions:

Heat olive oil in a large skillet over medium heat. Add chopped onion and garlic, sauté until softened.
Add ground beef to the skillet, breaking it apart with a spoon. Cook until browned.
Stir in grated carrot and chopped celery. Cook for a few minutes until vegetables are tender.
Pour in crushed tomatoes, tomato paste, beef broth, and red wine (if using). Mix well.
Season with dried oregano, dried basil, salt, and pepper. Reduce heat to low, cover, and simmer for at least 30 minutes (longer for richer flavor).
Meanwhile, cook spaghetti according to package instructions. Drain and set aside.
Once the Bolognese sauce has simmered, taste and adjust seasoning if needed.
Serve the Bolognese sauce over the cooked spaghetti. Garnish with grated Parmesan cheese.
Enjoy your homemade Spaghetti Bolognese!

Margherita Pizza

Ingredients:

- 1 pizza dough (store-bought or homemade)
- 1 cup tomato sauce (preferably San Marzano tomatoes)
- 8 ounces fresh mozzarella cheese, sliced
- Fresh basil leaves
- Extra-virgin olive oil
- Salt and pepper to taste

Instructions:

Preheat your oven to the highest temperature it can go (usually around 475-500°F or 245-260°C). If you have a pizza stone, place it in the oven during preheating.
Roll out the pizza dough on a lightly floured surface to your desired thickness.
If using a pizza stone, carefully transfer the rolled-out dough onto a pizza peel or an inverted baking sheet dusted with flour or cornmeal.
Spread the tomato sauce evenly over the pizza dough, leaving a small border around the edges.
Arrange slices of fresh mozzarella on top of the sauce.
Season the pizza with salt and pepper to taste.
Transfer the pizza to the preheated oven or onto the preheated pizza stone, if using. Bake for about 10-12 minutes or until the crust is golden and the cheese is bubbly and slightly browned.
Once out of the oven, sprinkle fresh basil leaves over the hot pizza.
Drizzle with extra-virgin olive oil.
Slice and serve immediately, enjoying the classic simplicity of Margherita Pizza!

Risotto alla Milanese

Ingredients:

- 1 1/2 cups Arborio rice
- 1/2 cup dry white wine
- 4 cups chicken or vegetable broth, kept warm
- 1 small onion, finely chopped
- 2 tablespoons unsalted butter
- 2 tablespoons olive oil
- 1/2 cup grated Parmesan cheese
- 1/2 teaspoon saffron threads
- Salt and pepper to taste

Instructions:

In a small bowl, soak the saffron threads in a couple of tablespoons of warm water.
In a large, shallow pan, heat 1 tablespoon of butter and 1 tablespoon of olive oil over medium heat.
Add the chopped onion and sauté until it becomes translucent.
Add the Arborio rice to the pan and toast it for a couple of minutes until the edges become slightly translucent.
Pour in the dry white wine and stir until most of the liquid has evaporated.
Start adding the warm broth, one ladle at a time, stirring frequently. Allow the liquid to be absorbed before adding more.
After about 15 minutes, add the saffron and its soaking liquid to the risotto.
Continue adding the broth and stirring until the rice is creamy and cooked to al dente texture.
Once the rice is cooked, stir in the remaining tablespoon of butter and the grated Parmesan cheese. Season with salt and pepper to taste.
Remove the risotto from heat and let it rest for a minute or two.
Serve the Risotto alla Milanese hot, garnishing with additional Parmesan if desired.

Enjoy the rich and flavorful Risotto alla Milanese!

Tiramisu

Ingredients:

- 6 egg yolks
- 1 cup granulated sugar
- 1 1/4 cups mascarpone cheese
- 1 3/4 cups heavy cream
- 1 cup strong brewed coffee, cooled
- 1/4 cup coffee liqueur (e.g., Kahlúa)
- 24-30 ladyfinger cookies (savoiardi)
- Unsweetened cocoa powder, for dusting

Instructions:

In a large mixing bowl, whisk together the egg yolks and sugar until the mixture becomes pale and slightly thickened.
Add the mascarpone cheese to the egg yolk mixture and beat until well combined and smooth.
In a separate bowl, whip the heavy cream until stiff peaks form.
Gently fold the whipped cream into the mascarpone mixture until smooth and well combined.
In a shallow dish, combine the brewed coffee and coffee liqueur.
Dip each ladyfinger into the coffee mixture, making sure not to soak them too much.
Arrange a layer of dipped ladyfingers in the bottom of a serving dish or individual glasses.
Spread half of the mascarpone mixture over the layer of ladyfingers.
Repeat the process with another layer of dipped ladyfingers and the remaining mascarpone mixture.
Cover the dish and refrigerate for at least 4 hours, preferably overnight, to allow the flavors to meld and the dessert to set.
Before serving, dust the top of the tiramisu with unsweetened cocoa powder using a fine sieve.
Serve chilled and enjoy this classic Italian Tiramisu!

Note: Traditional Tiramisu does not include raw eggs, but if you have concerns about consuming raw eggs, consider using pasteurized eggs or using an alternative recipe that does not include them.

Fettuccine Alfredo

Ingredients:

- 1 lb fettuccine pasta
- 1 cup unsalted butter
- 1 cup heavy cream
- 1 1/2 cups grated Parmesan cheese
- Salt and black pepper to taste
- Chopped parsley for garnish (optional)

Instructions:

Cook the fettuccine pasta according to the package instructions until al dente. Reserve about 1 cup of pasta cooking water before draining.
In a large skillet over medium heat, melt the butter.
Pour in the heavy cream, stirring constantly, and bring it to a simmer. Reduce the heat to low.
Gradually add the grated Parmesan cheese to the cream and butter mixture, stirring continuously to melt the cheese and create a smooth sauce.
If the sauce is too thick, add some of the reserved pasta cooking water a little at a time until you reach the desired consistency.
Season the Alfredo sauce with salt and black pepper to taste. Remember that Parmesan cheese is salty, so be cautious with the amount of additional salt.
Add the cooked fettuccine to the sauce, tossing to coat the pasta evenly.
Continue to cook for a few minutes until the pasta is well coated and heated through.
Serve the Fettuccine Alfredo hot, garnished with chopped parsley if desired.

Enjoy the creamy and indulgent Fettuccine Alfredo!

Osso Buco

Ingredients:

- 4 veal shanks, each about 1 1/2 inches thick
- Salt and pepper to taste
- All-purpose flour, for dredging
- 4 tablespoons olive oil
- 1 onion, finely chopped
- 2 carrots, finely chopped
- 2 celery stalks, finely chopped
- 4 cloves garlic, minced
- 1 cup dry white wine
- 1 can (14 oz) crushed tomatoes
- 1 cup chicken or beef broth
- 1 teaspoon dried oregano
- 1 teaspoon dried thyme
- 1 bay leaf
- Gremolata (optional for garnish):
    - Zest of 1 lemon
    - 2 tablespoons chopped fresh parsley
    - 1 clove garlic, minced

Instructions:

Preheat the oven to 375°F (190°C).

Season the veal shanks with salt and pepper, then dredge them in flour, shaking off any excess.

In a large, oven-safe pot or Dutch oven, heat the olive oil over medium-high heat. Brown the veal shanks on all sides, about 4-5 minutes per side. Remove them from the pot and set aside.

In the same pot, add chopped onion, carrots, celery, and minced garlic. Sauté until the vegetables are softened.

Pour in the dry white wine, scraping the bottom of the pot to release any browned bits.

Add crushed tomatoes, broth, dried oregano, dried thyme, and the bay leaf. Stir well.

Return the browned veal shanks to the pot, nestling them into the sauce.

Cover the pot and transfer it to the preheated oven. Bake for about 2 hours or until the meat is tender and falling off the bone.

While the Osso Buco is cooking, prepare the gremolata by mixing together lemon zest, chopped parsley, and minced garlic.

Once done, remove the pot from the oven. Taste and adjust the seasoning if needed.

Serve the Osso Buco hot, garnished with gremolata if desired. It pairs well with risotto, mashed potatoes, or crusty bread.

Enjoy this classic Italian Osso Buco!

Caprese Salad

Ingredients:

- 4 large ripe tomatoes, sliced
- 1 pound fresh mozzarella cheese, sliced
- Fresh basil leaves
- Extra-virgin olive oil
- Balsamic glaze (optional)
- Salt and pepper to taste

Instructions:

Arrange alternating slices of tomatoes and mozzarella on a serving platter or individual plates.
Tuck fresh basil leaves between the tomato and mozzarella slices.
Drizzle extra-virgin olive oil over the salad, ensuring it coats the tomatoes and mozzarella evenly.
If desired, drizzle balsamic glaze over the salad for added flavor.
Season the Caprese salad with salt and pepper to taste.
Serve immediately to preserve the freshness of the ingredients.

Enjoy the simple and refreshing flavors of Caprese Salad!

Eggplant Parmesan

Ingredients:

- 2 large eggplants, sliced into 1/2-inch rounds
- Salt
- 2 cups all-purpose flour
- 4 large eggs, beaten
- 2 cups breadcrumbs
- 1 cup grated Parmesan cheese
- Olive oil for frying
- 4 cups marinara sauce
- 2 cups shredded mozzarella cheese
- Fresh basil leaves for garnish (optional)

Instructions:

Sprinkle salt on the eggplant slices and let them sit for about 30 minutes to draw out excess moisture. Pat them dry with paper towels.
Set up a breading station with three shallow bowls: one with flour, one with beaten eggs, and one with a mixture of breadcrumbs and grated Parmesan.
Dredge each eggplant slice in the flour, then dip into the beaten eggs, and coat with the breadcrumb and Parmesan mixture.
In a large skillet, heat olive oil over medium heat. Fry the breaded eggplant slices until golden brown on both sides. Place them on paper towels to drain excess oil.
Preheat the oven to 375°F (190°C).
In a baking dish, spread a thin layer of marinara sauce. Arrange a layer of fried eggplant slices on top.
Pour more marinara sauce over the eggplant and sprinkle with shredded mozzarella cheese.
Repeat the layers until all the eggplant slices are used, finishing with a layer of sauce and mozzarella on top.
Bake in the preheated oven for about 25-30 minutes or until the cheese is melted and bubbly.
Let the Eggplant Parmesan rest for a few minutes before serving.
Garnish with fresh basil leaves if desired.

Serve this delicious Eggplant Parmesan with a side of pasta or a green salad. Enjoy!

Minestrone Soup

Ingredients:

- 2 tablespoons olive oil
- 1 onion, diced
- 2 carrots, diced
- 2 celery stalks, diced
- 3 cloves garlic, minced
- 1 zucchini, diced
- 1 yellow squash, diced
- 1 cup green beans, cut into bite-sized pieces
- 1 can (15 oz) diced tomatoes
- 1 can (15 oz) kidney beans, drained and rinsed
- 1/2 cup small pasta (e.g., ditalini or small elbow macaroni)
- 6 cups vegetable or chicken broth
- 1 teaspoon dried oregano
- 1 teaspoon dried basil
- 1/2 teaspoon dried thyme
- Salt and pepper to taste
- 2 cups fresh spinach or kale, chopped
- Grated Parmesan cheese for serving

Instructions:

In a large pot, heat olive oil over medium heat. Add diced onion, carrots, and celery. Sauté until the vegetables are softened.
Add minced garlic and cook for an additional minute until fragrant.
Stir in diced zucchini, yellow squash, green beans, diced tomatoes, and kidney beans.
Pour in the vegetable or chicken broth and bring the mixture to a simmer.
Add dried oregano, dried basil, dried thyme, salt, and pepper. Adjust the seasonings to taste.
Add the small pasta to the pot and cook according to package instructions until al dente.
Just before serving, stir in the chopped spinach or kale and cook until wilted.
Taste the Minestrone Soup and adjust the seasoning if needed.
Ladle the soup into bowls and serve hot, garnished with grated Parmesan cheese.

Enjoy this hearty and nutritious Minestrone Soup!

Ravioli with Tomato Sauce

Ingredients:

- 1 package (about 1 lb) of your favorite ravioli (cheese, spinach, or meat-filled)
- 2 tablespoons olive oil
- 3 cloves garlic, minced
- 1 can (28 oz) crushed tomatoes
- 1 teaspoon dried oregano
- 1 teaspoon dried basil
- Salt and pepper to taste
- Pinch of red pepper flakes (optional)
- Fresh basil or parsley for garnish
- Grated Parmesan cheese for serving

Instructions:

Cook the ravioli according to the package instructions in a large pot of salted boiling water. Drain and set aside.
In a large skillet, heat olive oil over medium heat. Add minced garlic and sauté until fragrant but not browned.
Pour in the crushed tomatoes and bring the sauce to a simmer.
Add dried oregano, dried basil, salt, pepper, and red pepper flakes if using. Stir well to combine.
Simmer the tomato sauce for about 10-15 minutes, allowing the flavors to meld and the sauce to thicken slightly.
Add the cooked ravioli to the tomato sauce and gently toss to coat the pasta with the sauce.
Taste and adjust the seasoning if needed.
Serve the Ravioli with Tomato Sauce in individual bowls, garnished with fresh basil or parsley and grated Parmesan cheese.

Enjoy this quick and delicious Ravioli with Tomato Sauce!

Gnocchi

Ingredients:

- 2 pounds potatoes (about 4 medium-sized potatoes)
- 2 cups all-purpose flour, plus more for dusting
- 1 large egg
- Salt

Instructions:

Wash and peel the potatoes. Cut them into uniform-sized chunks.
Place the potato chunks in a large pot, cover with water, and add a pinch of salt.
Bring to a boil and cook until the potatoes are fork-tender.
Drain the potatoes and let them cool for a few minutes.
Rice or mash the potatoes while they are still warm, ensuring there are no lumps.
Allow the mashed potatoes to cool completely.
Once cooled, create a mound with the mashed potatoes on a clean, floured surface.
In the center of the mound, make a well and add the beaten egg.
Gradually incorporate the flour into the potato mixture, using your hands, until you form a dough. Be careful not to over-knead.
Divide the dough into smaller sections and roll each section into a long rope, about 1/2 inch in diameter.
Cut the ropes into bite-sized pieces, forming the gnocchi. Optionally, you can use a fork to create ridges on the gnocchi.
Bring a large pot of salted water to a boil.
Drop the gnocchi into the boiling water in batches. Once they float to the surface, let them cook for an additional 1-2 minutes.
Use a slotted spoon to transfer the cooked gnocchi to a serving dish.
Serve the gnocchi with your favorite sauce, such as tomato sauce, pesto, or browned butter with sage.

Enjoy your homemade gnocchi!

Pasta Carbonara

Ingredients:

- 1 lb (450g) spaghetti or your favorite pasta
- 2 tablespoons olive oil
- 1/2 lb (225g) pancetta or guanciale, diced
- 4 large eggs
- 1 cup grated Pecorino Romano cheese
- 1 cup grated Parmesan cheese
- 3 cloves garlic, minced (optional)
- Salt and black pepper to taste
- Fresh parsley, chopped, for garnish

Instructions:

Cook the pasta in a large pot of salted boiling water according to the package instructions until al dente. Reserve about 1 cup of pasta cooking water before draining.

While the pasta is cooking, heat olive oil in a large skillet over medium heat. Add the diced pancetta or guanciale and cook until crispy. If using garlic, add it to the skillet during the last minute of cooking, being careful not to burn it.

In a bowl, whisk together the eggs, grated Pecorino Romano, and grated Parmesan cheese until well combined.

Once the pasta is cooked, drain it and immediately transfer it to the skillet with the pancetta or guanciale. Toss to coat the pasta with the rendered fat.

Remove the skillet from the heat and quickly pour the egg and cheese mixture over the pasta, tossing vigorously to create a creamy sauce. If needed, add some of the reserved pasta cooking water to achieve the desired consistency.

Season with salt and plenty of black pepper to taste.

Garnish the Pasta Carbonara with chopped fresh parsley.

Serve immediately, ensuring the pasta is hot, and enjoy the classic flavors of Pasta Carbonara!

Note: Traditional Carbonara uses Pecorino Romano cheese, but you can adjust the ratio of Pecorino to Parmesan based on your preference.

Cannoli

Ingredients:

For the Cannoli Shells:

- 2 cups all-purpose flour
- 2 tablespoons granulated sugar
- 1/4 teaspoon salt
- 2 tablespoons unsalted butter, softened
- 1/2 cup white wine
- 1 egg white (for sealing)

For the Cannoli Filling:

- 2 cups ricotta cheese, drained
- 1 cup powdered sugar
- 1 teaspoon vanilla extract
- 1/4 cup mini chocolate chips
- 1/4 cup chopped pistachios (optional)
- Powdered sugar, for dusting

Instructions:

For the Cannoli Shells:

In a large bowl, whisk together the flour, sugar, and salt.
Add the softened butter and mix until the mixture is crumbly.
Gradually add the white wine and mix until the dough comes together. Knead the dough on a lightly floured surface until smooth.
Wrap the dough in plastic wrap and let it rest at room temperature for at least 30 minutes.
Roll out the dough on a floured surface to about 1/8 inch thickness. Cut out rounds using a 4-inch cookie cutter.
Wrap each round of dough around a cannoli tube, sealing the edge with a little egg white.
Heat oil in a deep fryer or large, deep pan to 350°F (175°C).

Fry the cannoli shells, a few at a time, until golden brown. Use tongs to remove them and place them on a paper towel-lined tray to cool.

For the Cannoli Filling:

In a bowl, mix the drained ricotta cheese, powdered sugar, and vanilla extract until smooth.
Fold in the mini chocolate chips and chopped pistachios, if using.
Place the filling in a piping bag.
Once the cannoli shells are completely cool, pipe the ricotta filling into each end of the shells.
Dust the filled cannoli with powdered sugar.
Serve immediately and enjoy your homemade Cannoli!

Note: It's best to fill the cannoli just before serving to keep the shells crispy.

Pesto Genovese

Ingredients:

- 2 cups fresh basil leaves, packed
- 1/2 cup grated Parmesan cheese
- 1/2 cup pine nuts or walnuts
- 3 garlic cloves, peeled
- 1 cup extra-virgin olive oil
- Salt, to taste
- 1/2 cup grated Pecorino Romano cheese (optional)

Instructions:

In a food processor, combine the fresh basil, grated Parmesan cheese, pine nuts or walnuts, and peeled garlic cloves.
Pulse the ingredients until they are finely chopped.
With the food processor running, slowly pour in the olive oil in a steady stream until the mixture becomes a smooth paste.
Stop the food processor and scrape down the sides with a spatula to ensure all ingredients are well incorporated.
Add salt to taste and pulse briefly to mix.
If using, add the grated Pecorino Romano cheese and pulse a few times to combine. Adjust the consistency with more olive oil if needed.
Taste the pesto and adjust the salt if necessary.
Transfer the Pesto Genovese to a jar or airtight container.
If not using immediately, you can top the pesto with a thin layer of olive oil to prevent it from oxidizing.
Serve the pesto with your favorite pasta, as a sandwich spread, or as a topping for grilled meats or vegetables.

Enjoy the vibrant flavors of homemade Pesto Genovese!

Lasagna

Ingredients:

For the Meat Sauce:

- 1 lb (450g) ground beef
- 1/2 lb (225g) ground pork or Italian sausage
- 1 onion, finely chopped
- 3 cloves garlic, minced
- 1 can (28 oz) crushed tomatoes
- 1 can (14 oz) tomato sauce
- 2 tablespoons tomato paste
- 1/2 cup red wine (optional)
- 2 teaspoons dried oregano
- 2 teaspoons dried basil
- Salt and black pepper to taste

For the Ricotta Filling:

- 2 cups ricotta cheese
- 1 cup grated Parmesan cheese
- 1 egg
- 2 tablespoons fresh parsley, chopped
- Salt and black pepper to taste

Other Ingredients:

- 12 lasagna noodles, cooked al dente
- 3 cups shredded mozzarella cheese
- 1 cup grated Parmesan cheese
- Fresh basil or parsley for garnish (optional)

Instructions:

For the Meat Sauce:

In a large skillet, brown the ground beef and pork or sausage over medium-high heat, breaking it apart with a spoon.

Add chopped onion and garlic, and sauté until the onion is softened.

Pour in crushed tomatoes, tomato sauce, and tomato paste. Stir well.

Add red wine (if using), dried oregano, dried basil, salt, and black pepper. Simmer the sauce for at least 30 minutes, allowing the flavors to meld. Adjust seasoning as needed.

For the Ricotta Filling:

In a bowl, combine ricotta cheese, grated Parmesan cheese, egg, chopped parsley, salt, and black pepper. Mix until well combined.

Assembling the Lasagna:

Preheat the oven to 375°F (190°C).

In a baking dish, spread a thin layer of the meat sauce.

Place a layer of cooked lasagna noodles over the sauce.

Spread half of the ricotta filling over the noodles.

Sprinkle a layer of shredded mozzarella and grated Parmesan cheese over the ricotta.

Repeat the layers, finishing with a layer of meat sauce and a generous amount of shredded mozzarella.

Cover the baking dish with aluminum foil and bake in the preheated oven for about 25-30 minutes.

Remove the foil and continue baking for an additional 10-15 minutes or until the cheese is melted and bubbly.

Let the lasagna rest for 10-15 minutes before slicing.

Garnish with fresh basil or parsley if desired.

Serve this delicious Italian Lasagna hot and enjoy!

Bruschetta

Ingredients:

- Baguette or Italian bread, sliced
- 4-5 ripe tomatoes, diced
- 2 cloves garlic, minced
- Fresh basil leaves, chopped
- 1/4 cup extra-virgin olive oil
- 1 teaspoon balsamic vinegar (optional)
- Salt and black pepper to taste

Instructions:

Preheat the oven to 375°F (190°C).
Arrange the sliced baguette or Italian bread on a baking sheet. Drizzle with a little olive oil and toast in the oven until the edges are golden brown. You can also grill the bread for added flavor.
In a bowl, combine the diced tomatoes, minced garlic, chopped basil, extra-virgin olive oil, and balsamic vinegar (if using). Mix well.
Season the tomato mixture with salt and black pepper to taste. Adjust the seasoning as needed.
Allow the tomato mixture to marinate for at least 15-20 minutes to let the flavors meld.
Once the bread slices are toasted, remove them from the oven and let them cool slightly.
Spoon the tomato mixture generously over each bread slice.
Serve the bruschetta immediately as an appetizer or snack.

Enjoy this simple and delicious Bruschetta as a refreshing starter!

Veal Saltimbocca

Ingredients:

- 4 veal scaloppine (thinly sliced veal cutlets)
- Salt and black pepper to taste
- 4 slices prosciutto
- 8 fresh sage leaves
- All-purpose flour, for dredging
- 2 tablespoons unsalted butter
- 2 tablespoons olive oil
- 1/2 cup dry white wine
- 1/2 cup chicken broth
- 1 lemon, sliced (for garnish)

Instructions:

Season each veal scaloppine with salt and black pepper.

Place a slice of prosciutto on top of each veal scaloppine, and then add two fresh sage leaves on top of the prosciutto.

Secure the prosciutto and sage in place by gently pressing them onto the veal or using toothpicks.

Dredge each veal scaloppine in flour, shaking off any excess.

In a large skillet, heat the butter and olive oil over medium-high heat.

Add the veal scaloppine to the skillet, prosciutto side down. Cook for about 2-3 minutes until the prosciutto is crispy. Carefully flip the veal and cook the other side for an additional 2-3 minutes until the veal is cooked through.

Remove the veal from the skillet and set it aside on a plate.

Pour the white wine into the skillet, scraping up any browned bits from the bottom. Allow the wine to reduce for a minute or two.

Add the chicken broth to the skillet and bring the mixture to a simmer.

Return the veal to the skillet and cook for an additional 2 minutes in the sauce until it is heated through.

Transfer the veal saltimbocca to a serving platter. Spoon the sauce over the veal. Garnish with lemon slices.

Serve the Veal Saltimbocca hot, and enjoy this classic Italian dish!

Cioppino

Ingredients:

- 2 tablespoons olive oil
- 1 onion, chopped
- 1 fennel bulb, thinly sliced
- 3 cloves garlic, minced
- 1/2 teaspoon red pepper flakes (adjust to taste)
- 1 cup dry white wine
- 1 can (28 oz) crushed tomatoes
- 1 can (14 oz) diced tomatoes
- 4 cups fish or seafood broth
- 1 bay leaf
- 1 teaspoon dried oregano
- 1 teaspoon dried thyme
- Salt and black pepper to taste
- 1 pound mixed seafood (such as shrimp, mussels, clams, scallops, and fish fillets)
- 1/2 cup fresh parsley, chopped
- Crusty bread for serving

Instructions:

In a large pot, heat the olive oil over medium heat. Add chopped onion, sliced fennel, and minced garlic. Sauté until the vegetables are softened.
Add red pepper flakes and continue to sauté for another minute.
Pour in the white wine and bring it to a simmer. Allow it to cook for a couple of minutes to reduce slightly.
Add crushed tomatoes, diced tomatoes, fish or seafood broth, bay leaf, dried oregano, dried thyme, salt, and black pepper. Stir well to combine.
Bring the mixture to a boil and then reduce the heat to low. Let it simmer for about 20-30 minutes to allow the flavors to meld.
Taste the broth and adjust the seasoning if needed.
Add the mixed seafood to the pot, ensuring that the seafood is submerged in the broth. Cook for about 5-10 minutes or until the seafood is cooked through.
Discard the bay leaf.
Stir in chopped fresh parsley.
Serve the Cioppino hot in bowls, with crusty bread on the side for dipping.

Enjoy this flavorful and hearty Italian-American seafood stew!

Amatriciana Sauce

Ingredients:

- 2 tablespoons olive oil
- 1/2 pound (225g) guanciale or pancetta, diced
- 1 onion, finely chopped
- 3 cloves garlic, minced
- 1/2 teaspoon red pepper flakes (adjust to taste)
- 1 can (28 oz) crushed tomatoes
- Salt and black pepper to taste
- 1/2 cup Pecorino Romano cheese, grated
- 1 pound (450g) bucatini or spaghetti pasta
- Fresh parsley, chopped (for garnish)

Instructions:

In a large skillet, heat olive oil over medium heat. Add the diced guanciale or pancetta and sauté until it becomes crispy and golden brown.
Add the finely chopped onion to the skillet and cook until it becomes translucent.
Stir in the minced garlic and red pepper flakes, and sauté for an additional minute until fragrant.
Pour in the crushed tomatoes and bring the mixture to a simmer. Reduce the heat to low and let it simmer for about 15-20 minutes, allowing the flavors to meld.
Season the Amatriciana sauce with salt and black pepper to taste.
While the sauce is simmering, cook the pasta in a large pot of salted boiling water according to the package instructions until al dente.
Drain the pasta and reserve about 1/2 cup of pasta cooking water.
Toss the cooked pasta with the Amatriciana sauce, adding a little pasta cooking water if needed to reach the desired consistency.
Stir in the grated Pecorino Romano cheese, ensuring it melts into the sauce.
Serve the Amatriciana Sauce-coated pasta in individual bowls, garnished with fresh chopped parsley.

Enjoy this classic Roman pasta dish with bold flavors!

Polenta

Ingredients:

- 1 cup coarse or medium-grind polenta
- 4 cups water
- 1 teaspoon salt
- 2 tablespoons unsalted butter
- 1/2 cup grated Parmesan cheese (optional)
- Salt and black pepper to taste

Instructions:

In a large saucepan, bring 4 cups of water to a boil.
Gradually whisk in the polenta, stirring continuously to avoid lumps.
Add salt to the polenta and reduce the heat to low.
Simmer the polenta, stirring frequently, until it thickens. This may take 20-30 minutes depending on the type of polenta you're using.
Once the polenta is thickened and cooked to your desired consistency, stir in the unsalted butter.
If using, mix in grated Parmesan cheese for added creaminess. Season with salt and black pepper to taste.
Continue to cook and stir the polenta for an additional 2-3 minutes to ensure it's well combined and creamy.
Remove the polenta from the heat.
Serve the creamy polenta hot as a side dish. It pairs well with various sauces, stews, or grilled vegetables.

Enjoy this comforting and versatile dish!

Arancini

Ingredients:

For the Risotto:

- 1 cup Arborio rice
- 1/2 cup dry white wine
- 4 cups chicken or vegetable broth, heated
- 1 onion, finely chopped
- 2 tablespoons olive oil
- 1/2 cup grated Parmesan cheese
- Salt and black pepper to taste

For the Filling and Coating:

- Mozzarella cheese, cut into small cubes
- Breadcrumbs
- 2-3 eggs, beaten
- Vegetable oil for frying

Instructions:

For the Risotto:

In a large pan, heat the olive oil over medium heat. Add the chopped onion and sauté until it becomes translucent.
Add the Arborio rice to the pan and toast it for a couple of minutes until the edges become slightly translucent.
Pour in the white wine and stir until most of the liquid has evaporated.
Begin adding the warm broth, one ladle at a time, stirring frequently. Allow the liquid to be absorbed before adding more. Continue this process until the rice is creamy and cooked to al dente texture.
Stir in the grated Parmesan cheese and season with salt and black pepper to taste. Remove the risotto from heat and let it cool completely.

Assembling the Arancini:

Take a small portion of the cooled risotto in your hand and flatten it. Place a cube of mozzarella in the center.

Encase the mozzarella with the risotto, forming a ball. Ensure the mozzarella is completely covered.
Roll the risotto ball in breadcrumbs until it's well coated. Repeat this process for the remaining risotto.
Dip each risotto ball into beaten eggs and then roll it again in breadcrumbs to double coat.
Heat vegetable oil in a deep fryer or a large, deep pan to 350°F (175°C).
Fry the arancini in batches until they are golden brown and crispy on the outside. This usually takes about 3-4 minutes.
Use a slotted spoon to remove the arancini from the oil and place them on a paper towel-lined plate to drain excess oil.
Serve the arancini hot as an appetizer or snack.

Enjoy these delicious, golden-brown arancini with a gooey mozzarella center!

Panzanella

Ingredients:

- 4 cups stale Italian or rustic bread, cut into cubes
- 4 large ripe tomatoes, chopped
- 1 cucumber, peeled and sliced
- 1 red onion, thinly sliced
- 1 bell pepper (red or yellow), diced
- 1/2 cup Kalamata olives, pitted and halved
- 1/4 cup capers, drained
- 1/2 cup fresh basil leaves, torn
- 1/4 cup fresh parsley, chopped

For the Dressing:

- 1/3 cup extra-virgin olive oil
- 3 tablespoons red wine vinegar
- 1 teaspoon Dijon mustard
- 1 clove garlic, minced
- Salt and black pepper to taste

Instructions:

Preheat the oven to 375°F (190°C).
Place the bread cubes on a baking sheet and toast them in the oven until they are golden brown and crisp, about 10-15 minutes. Remove from the oven and let them cool.
In a large bowl, combine the chopped tomatoes, cucumber slices, thinly sliced red onion, diced bell pepper, olives, capers, torn basil leaves, and chopped parsley.
Add the toasted bread cubes to the bowl.
In a small bowl or jar, whisk together the olive oil, red wine vinegar, Dijon mustard, minced garlic, salt, and black pepper to make the dressing.
Pour the dressing over the salad and toss everything together until the bread cubes are coated and absorb some of the dressing.
Let the Panzanella sit for about 15-20 minutes before serving to allow the flavors to meld.

Taste and adjust the seasoning if needed.
Serve the Panzanella salad as a refreshing side dish or a light summer meal.

Enjoy this classic Italian bread salad!

Orecchiette with Broccoli Rabe

Ingredients:

- 1 lb (about 500g) orecchiette pasta
- 1 bunch broccoli rabe, washed and trimmed
- 3 tablespoons olive oil
- 4 cloves garlic, minced
- 1/2 teaspoon red pepper flakes (adjust to taste)
- Salt and black pepper to taste
- Grated Pecorino Romano cheese for serving

Instructions:

Bring a large pot of salted water to a boil. Add the orecchiette pasta and cook according to the package instructions until al dente.

While the pasta is cooking, blanch the broccoli rabe. Bring another pot of salted water to a boil and add the broccoli rabe. Cook for about 2-3 minutes until it's slightly tender but still vibrant green. Drain and set aside.

In a large skillet, heat the olive oil over medium heat. Add the minced garlic and red pepper flakes. Sauté for about 1 minute until the garlic is fragrant but not browned.

Add the blanched broccoli rabe to the skillet. Toss to coat it in the garlic-infused oil. Season with salt and black pepper to taste. Cook for an additional 2-3 minutes until the broccoli rabe is tender.

Once the orecchiette pasta is cooked, reserve about 1 cup of pasta cooking water and then drain the pasta.

Add the drained orecchiette to the skillet with the broccoli rabe. Toss everything together, adding some of the reserved pasta cooking water if needed to create a silky sauce.

Taste and adjust the seasoning if necessary.

Serve the Orecchiette with Broccoli Rabe hot, drizzled with a little extra olive oil, and topped with grated Pecorino Romano cheese.

Enjoy this simple and flavorful pasta dish!

Tiramisu

Ingredients:

- 6 egg yolks
- 1 cup granulated sugar
- 1 1/4 cups mascarpone cheese, softened
- 1 3/4 cups heavy cream
- 1 cup strong brewed coffee, cooled to room temperature
- 1/4 cup coffee liqueur (optional)
- 1 teaspoon vanilla extract
- Ladyfingers (about 24-30)
- Cocoa powder, for dusting

Instructions:

In a large bowl, whisk together the egg yolks and sugar until the mixture becomes pale and slightly thickened.

Add the softened mascarpone cheese to the egg yolk mixture. Beat until smooth and well combined.

In a separate bowl, whip the heavy cream until stiff peaks form.

Gently fold the whipped cream into the mascarpone mixture until fully incorporated.

In a shallow dish, combine the brewed coffee and coffee liqueur if using.

Dip each ladyfinger into the coffee mixture for a few seconds, making sure they are soaked but not overly soggy.

Arrange a layer of dipped ladyfingers in the bottom of a serving dish or individual serving glasses.

Spread half of the mascarpone mixture over the ladyfingers, smoothing it with a spatula.

Repeat the process with another layer of dipped ladyfingers and the remaining mascarpone mixture.

Cover the tiramisu and refrigerate for at least 4 hours or preferably overnight to allow the flavors to meld and the dessert to set.

Before serving, dust the top with cocoa powder using a fine-mesh sieve.

Serve the Tiramisu chilled and enjoy this classic Italian dessert!

Note: You can garnish with chocolate shavings or additional cocoa powder if desired. Adjust the amount of sugar and coffee liqueur based on your preference for sweetness and alcohol content.

Risotto ai Funghi

Ingredients:

- 1 1/2 cups Arborio rice
- 1/2 cup dry white wine
- 6 cups chicken or vegetable broth, kept warm
- 1/2 cup onion, finely chopped
- 2 tablespoons olive oil
- 2 tablespoons unsalted butter
- 2 cloves garlic, minced
- 1 lb (about 450g) mixed mushrooms (such as cremini, shiitake, or oyster), cleaned and sliced
- 1/2 cup grated Parmesan cheese
- Salt and black pepper to taste
- Fresh parsley, chopped (for garnish)

Instructions:

In a large skillet or pan, heat olive oil and 1 tablespoon of butter over medium heat.
Add the chopped onion and sauté until it becomes translucent.
Add the minced garlic and sauté for an additional minute until fragrant.
Add the sliced mushrooms to the skillet and cook until they release their moisture and become golden brown.
Remove a small portion of the mushrooms for garnish and set them aside.
Stir in the Arborio rice and cook for 1-2 minutes until the rice is well-coated with the oil and slightly toasted.
Pour in the white wine and stir until the wine is mostly absorbed.
Begin adding the warm chicken or vegetable broth, one ladle at a time, stirring frequently. Allow the liquid to be absorbed before adding more. Continue this process until the rice is creamy and cooked to al dente texture.
Stir in the remaining tablespoon of butter and grated Parmesan cheese. Season with salt and black pepper to taste.
Once the risotto is creamy and the rice is cooked, fold in the reserved sautéed mushrooms.
Remove the risotto from heat, cover, and let it rest for a couple of minutes.

Serve the Mushroom Risotto hot, garnished with fresh chopped parsley and additional Parmesan cheese if desired.

Enjoy the rich and savory flavors of this Mushroom Risotto!

Panna Cotta

Ingredients:

- 2 cups heavy cream
- 1/2 cup granulated sugar
- 1 teaspoon vanilla extract
- 1 packet (about 2 1/4 teaspoons) unflavored gelatin
- 3 tablespoons cold water
- Fresh berries or fruit compote for serving (optional)

Instructions:

In a saucepan, combine the heavy cream and sugar. Heat over medium heat, stirring occasionally, until the sugar dissolves. Do not bring it to a boil.
Remove the saucepan from heat and stir in the vanilla extract.
In a small bowl, sprinkle the gelatin over the cold water. Let it sit for about 5 minutes to soften.
After the gelatin has softened, gently heat it in the microwave for about 10 seconds or until it turns into a liquid.
Add the melted gelatin to the cream mixture and stir well to combine.
Strain the mixture through a fine-mesh sieve into a pouring jug to ensure a smooth texture.
Pour the Panna Cotta mixture into individual serving glasses or molds.
Refrigerate for at least 4 hours or preferably overnight to allow the Panna Cotta to set.
Once set, serve the Panna Cotta chilled, either in the glasses or by unmolding onto a plate.
Optionally, top the Panna Cotta with fresh berries or a fruit compote before serving.

Enjoy the delicate and creamy goodness of Panna Cotta!

Shrimp Scampi

Ingredients:

- 1 pound (about 450g) large shrimp, peeled and deveined
- Salt and black pepper to taste
- 1 pound linguine or spaghetti
- 4 tablespoons unsalted butter
- 4 tablespoons olive oil
- 4 cloves garlic, minced
- 1/2 teaspoon red pepper flakes (adjust to taste)
- 1/2 cup dry white wine
- Zest of 1 lemon
- Juice of 1 lemon
- 1/4 cup fresh parsley, chopped
- Grated Parmesan cheese for serving (optional)

Instructions:

Season the shrimp with salt and black pepper.
Cook the linguine or spaghetti in a large pot of salted boiling water until al dente. Drain and set aside.
In a large skillet, heat 2 tablespoons of butter and 2 tablespoons of olive oil over medium-high heat.
Add the minced garlic and red pepper flakes to the skillet. Sauté for about 1 minute until the garlic is fragrant but not browned.
Add the seasoned shrimp to the skillet and cook for 1-2 minutes on each side until they turn pink. Be careful not to overcook the shrimp. Remove them from the skillet and set aside.
In the same skillet, add the remaining 2 tablespoons of butter and 2 tablespoons of olive oil.
Pour in the white wine, scraping up any browned bits from the bottom of the skillet. Allow the wine to reduce for a couple of minutes.
Stir in the lemon zest and lemon juice.
Return the cooked shrimp to the skillet and toss them in the sauce to coat.
Add the cooked linguine or spaghetti to the skillet, tossing to combine and coat the pasta with the shrimp and sauce.
Season with additional salt and black pepper if needed.
Sprinkle chopped fresh parsley over the Shrimp Scampi and toss once more.

Optionally, serve with grated Parmesan cheese on top.

Enjoy this flavorful and quick Shrimp Scampi!

Prosciutto and Melon

Ingredients:

- Ripe cantaloupe or honeydew melon, chilled
- Prosciutto di Parma or your favorite cured ham

Instructions:

Cut the cantaloupe or honeydew melon in half and remove the seeds.
Using a melon baller or a knife, cut the melon into bite-sized pieces.
If you prefer a more elegant presentation, you can use a small cookie cutter to shape the melon into rounds.
Take slices of Prosciutto di Parma or your preferred cured ham.
Wrap each melon piece with a slice of prosciutto, securing it gently.
Arrange the Prosciutto-wrapped melon pieces on a serving platter.
Optionally, you can garnish with fresh mint leaves for added freshness.
Serve the Prosciutto and Melon as an appetizer or a light and refreshing snack.

Enjoy this classic and delightful combination of sweet melon and savory prosciutto!

Pasta Puttanesca

Ingredients:

- 1 pound (about 450g) spaghetti or your favorite pasta
- 3 tablespoons olive oil
- 4 cloves garlic, minced
- 6-8 anchovy fillets, chopped
- 1/2 teaspoon red pepper flakes (adjust to taste)
- 1 can (28 oz) crushed tomatoes
- 1/2 cup Kalamata olives, pitted and chopped
- 2 tablespoons capers, drained
- 2 tablespoons tomato paste
- Salt and black pepper to taste
- Fresh parsley, chopped (for garnish)
- Grated Parmesan cheese (optional, for serving)

Instructions:

Cook the pasta in a large pot of salted boiling water according to the package instructions until al dente. Drain and set aside.
In a large skillet, heat olive oil over medium heat. Add minced garlic, chopped anchovy fillets, and red pepper flakes. Sauté for 1-2 minutes until the garlic is fragrant and the anchovies have melted into the oil.
Stir in the crushed tomatoes, Kalamata olives, capers, and tomato paste. Bring the mixture to a simmer and let it cook for about 15-20 minutes, allowing the flavors to meld. Season with salt and black pepper to taste.
Toss the cooked pasta into the skillet with the sauce, ensuring it is well coated.
Garnish the Pasta Puttanesca with chopped fresh parsley.
Optionally, serve with grated Parmesan cheese on top.

Enjoy this flavorful and vibrant Pasta Puttanesca!

Zuppa Toscana

Ingredients:

- 1 pound (about 450g) Italian sausage, casings removed
- 1 large onion, diced
- 3 cloves garlic, minced
- 4 cups (about 1 liter) chicken broth
- 4 cups (about 1 liter) water
- 4 medium-sized potatoes, peeled and thinly sliced
- 1 bunch kale, stems removed and leaves chopped
- 1 cup heavy cream
- Salt and black pepper to taste
- Red pepper flakes (optional, for added heat)
- Grated Parmesan cheese for serving

Instructions:

In a large pot, brown the Italian sausage over medium-high heat, breaking it apart with a spoon as it cooks.
Add diced onion to the pot and sauté until the onion becomes translucent.
Stir in minced garlic and cook for an additional minute until fragrant.
Pour in chicken broth and water. Bring the mixture to a boil.
Add thinly sliced potatoes to the pot and simmer until the potatoes are tender, about 15-20 minutes.
Once the potatoes are cooked, reduce the heat to low.
Stir in chopped kale and let it simmer until the kale is wilted and cooked, about 5 minutes.
Add heavy cream to the pot and stir to combine. Season with salt and black pepper to taste.
If you like a bit of heat, you can add red pepper flakes to taste.
Allow the Zuppa Toscana to simmer for an additional 5-10 minutes to let the flavors meld.
Taste and adjust the seasoning if needed.
Serve the Zuppa Toscana hot, garnished with grated Parmesan cheese.

Enjoy this hearty and flavorful Tuscan soup!

Cacio e Pepe

Ingredients:

- 1 pound (about 450g) spaghetti or your preferred pasta
- 1 1/2 cups Pecorino Romano cheese, finely grated
- 1 tablespoon coarsely ground black pepper
- Salt for pasta water and to taste

Instructions:

Bring a large pot of salted water to a boil.
Add the spaghetti to the boiling water and cook according to the package instructions until al dente.
While the pasta is cooking, combine the finely grated Pecorino Romano cheese and coarsely ground black pepper in a bowl. Mix well.
When the pasta is almost done cooking, reserve about 1 cup of pasta cooking water, then drain the pasta.
Return the drained pasta to the pot.
Add a small amount of the reserved pasta cooking water to the Pecorino Romano and black pepper mixture, creating a thick paste.
Quickly toss the paste with the hot pasta, adding more pasta cooking water as needed to create a creamy sauce that coats the spaghetti evenly.
Continue tossing until the pasta is well coated and the sauce is smooth.
Serve the Cacio e Pepe immediately, garnished with additional black pepper and grated Pecorino Romano if desired.

Enjoy the simplicity and bold flavors of this classic Roman pasta dish!

Pistachio Gelato

Ingredients:

- 2 cups whole milk
- 1 cup heavy cream
- 3/4 cup granulated sugar
- 1/2 cup unsalted pistachios, shelled
- 1/2 teaspoon almond extract
- A pinch of salt
- Green food coloring (optional, for a vibrant color)

Instructions:

In a blender or food processor, blend the shelled pistachios until finely ground. You can leave some small chunks for texture if desired.

In a saucepan, combine the whole milk and heavy cream. Heat over medium heat until it begins to simmer, but do not let it boil.

In a separate bowl, whisk together the granulated sugar, ground pistachios, almond extract, and a pinch of salt.

Gradually add the pistachio mixture to the warm milk and cream, stirring continuously until the sugar dissolves. Continue to heat the mixture until it is just about to boil.

Remove the saucepan from heat and let the mixture cool to room temperature. Once cooled, cover the mixture and refrigerate for at least 4 hours or preferably overnight to allow the flavors to meld.

If you want a vibrant green color, you can add a few drops of green food coloring to the chilled mixture.

Pour the chilled mixture into an ice cream maker and churn according to the manufacturer's instructions.

Transfer the churned gelato to a lidded container and freeze for at least 4 hours or until firm.

Serve the Pistachio Gelato in bowls or cones.

Enjoy the rich and nutty flavor of homemade Pistachio Gelato!

Salted Cod (Baccalà)

Ingredients:

- 1 pound (about 450g) salted cod
- 2 cups all-purpose flour, for dredging
- 1 cup milk
- 2 large eggs
- Vegetable oil, for frying
- Fresh parsley, chopped (for garnish)
- Lemon wedges (for serving)

Instructions:

Rinse the salted cod under cold running water to remove excess salt. Pat it dry with paper towels.
Cut the salted cod into serving-sized pieces.
In a shallow dish, place the flour for dredging.
In another dish, whisk together the milk and eggs to create an egg wash.
Heat vegetable oil in a frying pan over medium-high heat.
Dredge each piece of salted cod in the flour, shaking off any excess.
Dip the floured cod into the egg wash, ensuring it is fully coated.
Carefully place the coated cod in the hot oil and fry until golden brown on each side, about 3-4 minutes per side. Adjust the heat as needed to prevent burning.
Once the cod is golden brown and cooked through, remove it from the oil and place it on a plate lined with paper towels to absorb excess oil.
Garnish the fried salted cod with chopped fresh parsley.
Serve the Salted Cod hot, with lemon wedges on the side.

Enjoy this traditional and flavorful dish!

Veal Marsala

Ingredients:

- 1 1/2 pounds veal scaloppine (thinly sliced veal cutlets)
- Salt and black pepper to taste
- 1/2 cup all-purpose flour, for dredging
- 4 tablespoons unsalted butter
- 4 tablespoons olive oil
- 1 cup cremini or button mushrooms, sliced
- 1/2 cup Marsala wine
- 1/2 cup chicken broth
- 1/4 cup fresh parsley, chopped (for garnish)
- Lemon wedges (for serving)

Instructions:

Season the veal scaloppine with salt and black pepper.
Dredge the veal in flour, shaking off any excess.
In a large skillet, heat 2 tablespoons of butter and 2 tablespoons of olive oil over medium-high heat.
Add the veal to the skillet and cook for about 2-3 minutes on each side, or until browned and cooked through. Cook in batches if necessary. Remove the veal from the skillet and set aside.
In the same skillet, add the remaining 2 tablespoons of butter and 2 tablespoons of olive oil.
Add the sliced mushrooms to the skillet and sauté until they are golden brown.
Pour in the Marsala wine, scraping up any browned bits from the bottom of the skillet. Allow the wine to reduce for a couple of minutes.
Add the chicken broth to the skillet and bring the mixture to a simmer.
Return the cooked veal to the skillet and let it simmer in the sauce for an additional 2-3 minutes to heat through.
Taste the sauce and adjust the seasoning if necessary.
Garnish the Veal Marsala with chopped fresh parsley.
Serve hot, with lemon wedges on the side.

Enjoy this classic Italian dish with its rich and flavorful Marsala wine sauce!

Pappardelle with Wild Boar Ragu

Ingredients:

For the Wild Boar Ragu:

- 1.5 pounds wild boar meat, diced
- Salt and black pepper to taste
- 2 tablespoons olive oil
- 1 onion, finely chopped
- 2 carrots, finely chopped
- 2 celery stalks, finely chopped
- 4 cloves garlic, minced
- 1 cup red wine
- 2 cans (28 oz each) crushed tomatoes
- 2 bay leaves
- 1 teaspoon dried thyme
- 1 teaspoon dried rosemary
- Salt and black pepper to taste

For the Pappardelle Pasta:

- 1 pound pappardelle pasta
- Salt for pasta water
- Grated Parmesan cheese (for serving)

Instructions:

For the Wild Boar Ragu:

Season the diced wild boar meat with salt and black pepper.
In a large Dutch oven or heavy pot, heat olive oil over medium-high heat.
Add the seasoned wild boar meat to the pot and brown on all sides. Remove the meat and set it aside.
In the same pot, add chopped onion, carrots, celery, and minced garlic. Sauté until the vegetables are softened.
Pour in the red wine, scraping up any browned bits from the bottom of the pot.
Add the crushed tomatoes, bay leaves, dried thyme, dried rosemary, and the browned wild boar meat back to the pot.

Bring the mixture to a simmer, then reduce the heat to low, cover, and let it simmer for at least 2-3 hours, stirring occasionally. The longer it simmers, the more tender and flavorful the ragu will be.

Season the ragu with salt and black pepper to taste. Remove the bay leaves.

For the Pappardelle Pasta:

Bring a large pot of salted water to a boil.
Cook the pappardelle pasta according to the package instructions until al dente.
Drain the pasta and toss it with a little olive oil to prevent sticking.

To Serve:

Plate the cooked pappardelle and ladle the wild boar ragu over the pasta.
Garnish with grated Parmesan cheese.
Serve hot and enjoy the rich flavors of Pappardelle with Wild Boar Ragu!

This dish is a hearty and comforting representation of traditional Italian cuisine.

Cannelloni

Ingredients:

For the Filling:

- 1 pound (about 450g) ricotta cheese
- 1 cup cooked spinach, chopped and drained well
- 1 cup grated Parmesan cheese
- 1 egg
- Salt and black pepper to taste
- Pinch of nutmeg (optional)

For the Tomato Sauce:

- 2 cans (28 oz each) crushed tomatoes
- 2 cloves garlic, minced
- 2 tablespoons olive oil
- 1 teaspoon dried oregano
- 1 teaspoon dried basil
- Salt and black pepper to taste

Other Ingredients:

- 12-16 cannelloni tubes
- 2 cups shredded mozzarella cheese
- Grated Parmesan cheese for topping

Instructions:

For the Filling:

In a bowl, combine ricotta cheese, cooked and chopped spinach, grated Parmesan cheese, egg, salt, black pepper, and nutmeg (if using). Mix well to form a smooth filling.

For the Tomato Sauce:

In a saucepan, heat olive oil over medium heat. Add minced garlic and sauté until fragrant.

Add crushed tomatoes, dried oregano, dried basil, salt, and black pepper. Simmer the sauce for about 20-30 minutes, stirring occasionally.

For Assembling:

Preheat the oven to 375°F (190°C).

Spread a thin layer of tomato sauce on the bottom of a baking dish.

Using a piping bag or a spoon, fill each cannelloni tube with the ricotta and spinach filling.

Arrange the filled cannelloni tubes in the baking dish.

Pour the remaining tomato sauce over the cannelloni, making sure they are well-covered.

Sprinkle shredded mozzarella cheese over the top.

Finish with a generous dusting of grated Parmesan cheese.

Bake in the preheated oven for about 25-30 minutes or until the cheese is golden and bubbly.

Allow the Cannelloni to rest for a few minutes before serving.

Serve this delicious Cannelloni hot and enjoy a taste of authentic Italian comfort food!

Calzone

Ingredients:

For the Dough:

- 2 1/4 teaspoons (1 packet) active dry yeast
- 1 cup warm water (110°F/43°C)
- 3 cups all-purpose flour
- 1 teaspoon sugar
- 1 teaspoon salt
- 2 tablespoons olive oil

For the Filling:

- 1 cup ricotta cheese
- 1 cup shredded mozzarella cheese
- 1/2 cup grated Parmesan cheese
- 1/2 cup tomato sauce
- 1/2 cup cooked and crumbled Italian sausage or pepperoni (optional)
- 1/4 cup chopped fresh basil or parsley
- Salt and black pepper to taste

For the Egg Wash:

- 1 egg, beaten

Instructions:

For the Dough:

In a small bowl, combine the warm water, sugar, and active dry yeast. Let it sit for about 5-10 minutes until it becomes frothy.
In a large mixing bowl, combine the flour and salt. Make a well in the center.
Pour the yeast mixture and olive oil into the well. Mix until a dough forms.
Knead the dough on a floured surface for about 5-7 minutes until it becomes smooth and elastic.

Place the dough in a lightly oiled bowl, cover it with a damp cloth, and let it rise in a warm place for 1-1.5 hours or until it doubles in size.

For the Filling:

In a bowl, mix together ricotta cheese, mozzarella cheese, Parmesan cheese, tomato sauce, Italian sausage or pepperoni (if using), chopped basil or parsley, salt, and black pepper.

Assembly:

Preheat the oven to 475°F (245°C).
Punch down the risen dough and divide it into equal portions for individual calzones.
Roll out each portion into a circle or oval shape on a floured surface.
Place a generous amount of the filling on one half of the rolled-out dough, leaving a border around the edges.
Fold the other half of the dough over the filling, creating a half-moon shape.
Press the edges together to seal the calzone. You can use a fork to crimp the edges.

Baking:

Place the assembled calzones on a baking sheet lined with parchment paper.
Brush the tops of the calzones with the beaten egg to create a golden crust.
Cut a small slit or poke a few holes on the top to allow steam to escape.
Bake in the preheated oven for about 12-15 minutes or until the calzones are golden brown.
Allow the calzones to cool for a few minutes before serving.

Serve these delicious calzones warm and enjoy the flavorful combination of crispy crust and cheesy filling!

Zabaione

Ingredients:

- 4 large egg yolks
- 1/4 cup granulated sugar
- 1/2 cup sweet Marsala wine
- Fresh berries or biscotti (for serving)

Instructions:

In a heatproof bowl, whisk together the egg yolks and sugar until well combined. Place the bowl over a pot of simmering water (double boiler), ensuring that the bottom of the bowl does not touch the water.

Gradually add the Marsala wine to the egg yolk mixture, whisking continuously. Continue whisking the mixture over the simmering water until it thickens and becomes frothy. This process may take about 8-10 minutes.

The zabaione is ready when it reaches a custard-like consistency, thick enough to coat the back of a spoon.

Remove the bowl from the heat and continue whisking for a minute or two as it cools slightly.

Serve the zabaione immediately in individual serving glasses or bowls.

Optionally, garnish with fresh berries or serve with biscotti on the side.

Enjoy this classic Italian dessert with its velvety texture and rich flavor!

Eggplant Caponata

Ingredients:

- 1 large eggplant, diced into small cubes
- 1/2 cup olive oil, divided
- 1 onion, finely chopped
- 2 celery stalks, finely chopped
- 1 red bell pepper, diced
- 1/2 cup green olives, pitted and sliced
- 1/4 cup capers, drained
- 2 tablespoons pine nuts, toasted
- 3 tablespoons red wine vinegar
- 2 tablespoons tomato paste
- 1 tablespoon sugar
- Salt and black pepper to taste
- Fresh parsley, chopped (for garnish)

Instructions:

Preheat the oven to 400°F (200°C).
Spread the diced eggplant on a baking sheet. Drizzle with 1/4 cup of olive oil and toss to coat. Roast in the preheated oven for about 20-25 minutes or until the eggplant is tender and golden brown. Stir occasionally during roasting.
In a large skillet, heat the remaining 1/4 cup of olive oil over medium heat.
Add the chopped onion and celery to the skillet. Sauté until they become soft and translucent.
Add the diced red bell pepper to the skillet and continue to sauté for an additional 3-4 minutes.
Stir in the sliced olives, drained capers, and toasted pine nuts. Cook for another 2 minutes.
In a small bowl, whisk together the red wine vinegar, tomato paste, sugar, salt, and black pepper.
Pour the vinegar mixture over the vegetables in the skillet. Stir to combine.
Add the roasted eggplant to the skillet and gently fold everything together.
Let the caponata simmer for about 10-15 minutes over low heat, allowing the flavors to meld.
Taste and adjust the seasoning if needed.
Remove the skillet from heat and let the caponata cool to room temperature.

Garnish with chopped fresh parsley before serving.
Serve the Eggplant Caponata as an appetizer, side dish, or atop crusty bread slices.

Enjoy the sweet and tangy flavors of this classic Sicilian dish!

Pasta Primavera

Ingredients:

- 12 ounces (340g) pasta of your choice (spaghetti, fettuccine, or penne)
- 2 tablespoons olive oil
- 3 cloves garlic, minced
- 1 small red onion, thinly sliced
- 1 bell pepper, thinly sliced
- 1 zucchini, thinly sliced
- 1 yellow squash, thinly sliced
- 1 carrot, julienned or thinly sliced
- 1 cup cherry tomatoes, halved
- 1 cup broccoli florets
- 1/2 cup frozen peas, thawed
- Salt and black pepper to taste
- 1/2 teaspoon red pepper flakes (optional)
- 1/2 cup grated Parmesan cheese
- Fresh basil or parsley, chopped (for garnish)
- Lemon wedges (for serving)

Instructions:

Cook the pasta according to the package instructions in a large pot of salted boiling water. Drain and set aside.
In a large skillet, heat olive oil over medium heat.
Add minced garlic and sliced red onion to the skillet. Sauté until the onion is softened.
Add the sliced bell pepper, zucchini, yellow squash, julienned carrot, cherry tomatoes, broccoli florets, and thawed peas to the skillet. Sauté for about 5-7 minutes or until the vegetables are tender-crisp.
Season the vegetables with salt, black pepper, and red pepper flakes (if using).
Add the cooked pasta to the skillet and toss everything together to combine.
Sprinkle grated Parmesan cheese over the pasta and vegetables. Toss again until the cheese is melted and coats the pasta.
Remove the skillet from heat.
Garnish with chopped fresh basil or parsley.
Serve the Pasta Primavera hot, with lemon wedges on the side.

Enjoy this colorful and vibrant pasta dish that highlights the flavors of fresh, seasonal vegetables!

Saffron Risotto

Ingredients:

- 1 1/2 cups Arborio rice
- 4 cups chicken or vegetable broth, kept warm
- 1/2 cup dry white wine
- 1 small onion, finely chopped
- 2 tablespoons unsalted butter
- 2 tablespoons olive oil
- 1/4 teaspoon saffron threads
- 1/2 cup grated Parmesan cheese
- Salt and black pepper to taste
- Fresh parsley, chopped (for garnish)

Instructions:

In a small bowl, steep the saffron threads in 2 tablespoons of warm water. Let it sit for about 10-15 minutes to release the flavor and color.
In a large skillet or saucepan, heat the olive oil and 1 tablespoon of butter over medium heat.
Add the finely chopped onion to the skillet and sauté until it becomes translucent.
Stir in the Arborio rice and cook for 1-2 minutes until the rice is well-coated with the oil.
Pour in the dry white wine and cook until it is mostly absorbed by the rice.
Begin adding the warm chicken or vegetable broth, one ladle at a time, stirring frequently. Allow the liquid to be absorbed before adding more. Continue this process until the rice is creamy and cooked to al dente texture.
Infuse the saffron water into the risotto by adding it to the pot along with the broth.
Continue stirring and adding broth until the rice is creamy and cooked to your desired consistency.
Stir in the remaining tablespoon of butter and grated Parmesan cheese. Season with salt and black pepper to taste.
Remove the saffron risotto from heat, cover, and let it rest for a couple of minutes.
Garnish with chopped fresh parsley.
Serve the Saffron Risotto hot, and enjoy the rich and aromatic flavors!

This luxurious saffron risotto is a perfect side dish or a main course that showcases the unique taste and color of saffron.

Porchetta

Ingredients:

For the Porchetta:

- 1 whole boneless pork belly (about 5-7 pounds)
- 1 pork loin (about 3-4 pounds)
- 6 cloves garlic, minced
- 1/4 cup fresh rosemary, chopped
- 1/4 cup fresh sage, chopped
- 2 tablespoons fennel seeds, crushed
- 1 tablespoon black pepper, coarsely ground
- Zest of 1 lemon
- Salt to taste
- Kitchen twine

For the Rub:

- 2 tablespoons olive oil
- 1 tablespoon fennel seeds, crushed
- 1 tablespoon black pepper, coarsely ground
- 1 teaspoon salt

Instructions:

Score the skin of the pork belly and pork loin with a sharp knife in a crosshatch pattern. Ensure not to cut too deeply into the meat.
In a bowl, combine the minced garlic, chopped rosemary, chopped sage, crushed fennel seeds, coarsely ground black pepper, lemon zest, and salt.
Lay the pork belly flat, skin side down. Rub half of the herb and spice mixture evenly over the meat.
Place the pork loin in the center of the pork belly.
Sprinkle the remaining herb and spice mixture over the pork loin.
Roll the pork belly around the pork loin, creating a cylindrical shape. Tie the porchetta with kitchen twine at 1-inch intervals to secure it.

In a small bowl, mix together olive oil, crushed fennel seeds, coarsely ground black pepper, and salt. Rub this mixture over the scored skin of the porchetta.

Place the porchetta on a rack in a roasting pan, skin side up.

Preheat the oven to 325°F (163°C).

Roast the porchetta in the preheated oven for about 3-4 hours or until the internal temperature reaches 145°F (63°C) for the pork loin and the skin is crispy.

Allow the porchetta to rest for about 20 minutes before carving.

Carve and serve the porchetta slices with your favorite side dishes.

Enjoy the succulent and flavorful Porchetta, a classic Italian roast with a crispy skin and aromatic herb stuffing!

Grilled Calamari

Ingredients:

- 1 pound (about 450g) fresh calamari tubes and tentacles, cleaned
- 2 tablespoons olive oil
- 2 cloves garlic, minced
- 1 teaspoon dried oregano
- Zest and juice of 1 lemon
- Salt and black pepper to taste
- Fresh parsley, chopped (for garnish)
- Lemon wedges (for serving)

Instructions:

If the calamari tubes are whole, slice them into rings. Leave smaller tentacles whole.
In a bowl, combine olive oil, minced garlic, dried oregano, lemon zest, lemon juice, salt, and black pepper to create a marinade.
Add the cleaned calamari to the marinade and toss to coat evenly. Let it marinate for at least 15-20 minutes.
Preheat the grill to medium-high heat.
Thread the calamari rings and tentacles onto skewers.
Place the calamari skewers on the preheated grill and cook for about 2-3 minutes per side or until the calamari is opaque and has grill marks.
Remove the grilled calamari from the skewers and place them on a serving platter.
Drizzle with any remaining marinade and sprinkle with fresh chopped parsley.
Serve the Grilled Calamari hot, with lemon wedges on the side.

Enjoy this simple and flavorful grilled calamari as an appetizer or part of a seafood feast!

Lemon Sorbet

Ingredients:

- 1 cup fresh lemon juice (about 4-6 lemons)
- 1 cup granulated sugar
- 2 cups water
- Zest of 1 lemon (optional, for extra flavor)

Instructions:

In a small saucepan, combine sugar and water. Heat over medium heat, stirring occasionally, until the sugar completely dissolves. Remove from heat and let it cool to room temperature.

In a bowl, combine the fresh lemon juice and the cooled sugar syrup. Add lemon zest if desired for an extra burst of flavor.

Pour the lemon mixture into an ice cream maker.

Churn the mixture according to the manufacturer's instructions until it reaches a slushy, frozen consistency.

Transfer the partially frozen sorbet into a lidded container.

Freeze the sorbet for at least 4 hours or until it is firm.

Before serving, let the sorbet sit at room temperature for a few minutes to soften slightly.

Scoop the Lemon Sorbet into bowls or cones.

Enjoy this refreshing and tangy Lemon Sorbet as a palate cleanser or a delightful summer treat!

Bagna Cauda

Ingredients:

- 1 cup extra-virgin olive oil
- 10-12 cloves garlic, minced
- 6-8 anchovy fillets, finely chopped
- 1/2 cup unsalted butter
- Fresh vegetables for dipping (e.g., broccoli, cauliflower, carrots, bell peppers, and celery)
- Bread for serving

Instructions:

In a saucepan over low heat, combine the olive oil, minced garlic, and finely chopped anchovies.
Cook the mixture gently, stirring occasionally, until the garlic becomes fragrant and the anchovies dissolve into the oil. This usually takes about 15-20 minutes. Be careful not to let the garlic brown.
Once the garlic and anchovies have infused the oil, add the unsalted butter to the saucepan. Stir until the butter is melted and well combined.
Continue to cook the Bagna Cauda for another 5-10 minutes, allowing the flavors to meld. The mixture should be warm and smooth.
Serve the Bagna Cauda in a heatproof dish or fondue pot, placed over a low flame to keep it warm.
Arrange a variety of fresh vegetables on a serving platter for dipping.
Provide chunks of bread for dipping as well.
To enjoy, dip the vegetables and bread into the warm Bagna Cauda, savoring the rich and flavorful combination.

Bagna Cauda is traditionally served as a communal dish, where everyone can gather around and enjoy the delightful flavors of the warm dip with an assortment of fresh vegetables and bread.

Pecorino Cheese with Honey

Ingredients:

- Pecorino cheese, sliced or in chunks
- Honey

Instructions:

Arrange slices or chunks of Pecorino cheese on a serving platter.
Drizzle honey over the Pecorino cheese, ensuring that each piece gets a touch of sweetness.
Serve the Pecorino cheese with honey immediately.
Optionally, you can garnish with fresh herbs, nuts, or dried fruits for added flavor and texture.
Enjoy this simple and delightful combination of Pecorino cheese and honey as a quick appetizer or part of a cheese board.

This pairing offers a wonderful balance of the salty, savory notes of Pecorino cheese with the natural sweetness of honey.

Sausage and Peppers

Ingredients:

- 1 pound Italian sausage links (sweet, hot, or a combination)
- 2 tablespoons olive oil
- 1 large onion, thinly sliced
- 2 bell peppers (any color), thinly sliced
- 3 cloves garlic, minced
- 1 can (14 ounces) crushed tomatoes
- 1 teaspoon dried oregano
- 1 teaspoon dried basil
- Salt and black pepper to taste
- Crushed red pepper flakes (optional, for added heat)
- Fresh parsley, chopped (for garnish)
- Sub rolls or crusty bread (for serving)

Instructions:

Preheat the oven to 375°F (190°C).
Prick the sausages with a fork to prevent them from bursting while cooking.
In an oven-safe skillet, heat olive oil over medium heat.
Add the sausages to the skillet and brown them on all sides. Remove the sausages from the skillet and set them aside.
In the same skillet, add sliced onions and bell peppers. Sauté until they are softened and slightly caramelized.
Add minced garlic to the skillet and sauté for an additional minute until fragrant.
Pour in the crushed tomatoes and add dried oregano, dried basil, salt, black pepper, and crushed red pepper flakes if desired. Stir to combine.
Return the browned sausages to the skillet, nestling them into the pepper and onion mixture.
Transfer the skillet to the preheated oven and bake for about 25-30 minutes or until the sausages are cooked through.
Remove the skillet from the oven and garnish with chopped fresh parsley.
Serve the sausage and peppers hot, either on its own or in sub rolls for sandwiches.

Enjoy this classic Italian-American dish that's bursting with flavors of sweet and savory peppers along with perfectly cooked sausages!

Farfalle with Salmon Cream Sauce

Ingredients:

- 12 ounces (340g) farfalle pasta
- 1 tablespoon olive oil
- 1 pound (about 450g) fresh salmon fillet, skinless and boneless, cut into bite-sized pieces
- Salt and black pepper to taste
- 2 tablespoons unsalted butter
- 3 cloves garlic, minced
- 1/2 cup dry white wine
- 1 cup heavy cream
- Zest and juice of 1 lemon
- 1/2 cup grated Parmesan cheese
- 1/4 cup fresh dill, chopped (plus extra for garnish)
- Lemon wedges (for serving)

Instructions:

Cook the farfalle pasta in a large pot of salted boiling water according to the package instructions until al dente. Drain and set aside.

In a large skillet, heat olive oil over medium-high heat.

Season the salmon pieces with salt and black pepper. Add the salmon to the skillet and cook for 2-3 minutes per side or until it's just cooked through. Remove the salmon from the skillet and set it aside.

In the same skillet, add butter and minced garlic. Sauté the garlic until it becomes fragrant.

Pour in the dry white wine and let it simmer for a minute to reduce slightly.

Add the heavy cream to the skillet, stirring continuously.

Stir in the lemon zest and juice.

Add the cooked farfalle pasta to the skillet and toss to coat the pasta with the creamy sauce.

Gently fold in the cooked salmon pieces.

Sprinkle grated Parmesan cheese over the pasta and stir until the cheese is melted and the sauce is creamy.

Remove the skillet from heat and stir in the chopped fresh dill.

Garnish with extra dill and serve the Farfalle with Salmon Cream Sauce hot, with lemon wedges on the side.

Enjoy this delicious pasta dish that combines the richness of salmon with a creamy and tangy lemon sauce!

Neapolitan Pizza

Ingredients:

For the Pizza Dough:

- 4 cups all-purpose flour (Tipo "00" flour is preferred)
- 1 1/2 teaspoons salt
- 1 teaspoon active dry yeast
- 1 1/2 cups warm water (about 110°F/43°C)
- 1 teaspoon sugar

For the Pizza Sauce:

- 1 can (28 ounces) whole San Marzano tomatoes
- 1-2 cloves garlic, minced
- Salt and black pepper to taste
- Fresh basil leaves

For Topping:

- Fresh mozzarella cheese, sliced
- Fresh basil leaves
- Extra-virgin olive oil

Instructions:

For the Pizza Dough:

In a small bowl, combine warm water, active dry yeast, and sugar. Let it sit for about 5 minutes until it becomes frothy.
In a large mixing bowl, combine flour and salt. Make a well in the center.
Pour the yeast mixture into the well. Mix until a dough forms.
Knead the dough on a floured surface for about 10-15 minutes until it becomes smooth and elastic.
Place the dough in a lightly oiled bowl, cover with a damp cloth, and let it rise in a warm place for 1-2 hours or until it doubles in size.

For the Pizza Sauce:

In a blender or food processor, blend the San Marzano tomatoes until smooth.
In a bowl, combine the tomato puree with minced garlic, salt, and black pepper.
Stir to combine.

Assembly and Baking:

Preheat your pizza oven or regular oven to the highest temperature possible (usually around 500-550°F or 260-290°C).
Divide the risen pizza dough into individual portions (about 8-10 ounces each) and shape them into balls. Let them rest for another 30 minutes.
On a floured surface, stretch and shape each dough ball into a round pizza crust.
Place the stretched dough on a pizza peel or parchment paper.
Spread a thin layer of the tomato sauce over the pizza dough.
Add slices of fresh mozzarella and scatter fresh basil leaves on top.
Drizzle with extra-virgin olive oil.
Transfer the pizza to the preheated oven or pizza oven and bake for about 8-10 minutes or until the crust is golden and the cheese is bubbly and slightly browned.
Remove the pizza from the oven, let it cool for a minute, and then slice.
Serve the Neapolitan Pizza hot and enjoy the authentic flavors of this classic pizza!

Note: For an authentic Neapolitan pizza experience, consider using a wood-fired pizza oven. Cooking times may vary depending on your oven.

Stracciatella Soup

Ingredients:

For the Broth:

- 6 cups chicken or vegetable broth
- 1 carrot, finely diced
- 1 celery stalk, finely diced
- 1 small onion, finely diced
- 2 cloves garlic, minced
- 1 bay leaf
- Salt and black pepper to taste

For the Egg Mixture (Stracciatella):

- 2 large eggs
- 1/2 cup grated Parmesan cheese
- 2 tablespoons fresh parsley, finely chopped
- Salt and black pepper to taste

Instructions:

For the Broth:

In a large pot, bring the chicken or vegetable broth to a simmer over medium heat.
Add the finely diced carrot, celery, onion, minced garlic, bay leaf, salt, and black pepper to the broth.
Simmer the broth for about 15-20 minutes or until the vegetables are tender.
Adjust the seasoning to taste and discard the bay leaf.

For the Egg Mixture (Stracciatella):

In a bowl, whisk together the eggs, grated Parmesan cheese, chopped fresh parsley, salt, and black pepper.

For Assembling:

Once the broth is simmering, use a fork to stir the broth in a circular motion.

While stirring, slowly pour the egg mixture into the simmering broth in a thin stream. The eggs will cook immediately, forming delicate strands.
Continue stirring for a minute or two until the egg mixture is fully incorporated into the broth.
Remove the pot from heat.
Ladle the Stracciatella Soup into bowls, making sure to get a good mix of broth and egg strands.
Serve the Stracciatella Soup hot, garnished with additional grated Parmesan cheese and fresh parsley if desired.

Enjoy this comforting and light Italian egg drop soup, perfect for a warming and nourishing meal!

Grilled Branzino

Ingredients:

- 2 whole branzino, gutted and scaled
- 2 tablespoons olive oil
- 4 cloves garlic, minced
- 1 lemon, sliced
- Fresh herbs (rosemary, thyme, or parsley)
- Salt and black pepper to taste
- Lemon wedges (for serving)

Instructions:

Preheat the grill to medium-high heat.
Make diagonal cuts on both sides of each branzino, about 2-3 cuts on each side.
This helps the fish cook more evenly and allows flavors to penetrate.
Rub the branzino with olive oil, ensuring it is well-coated on both sides.
Season the fish with minced garlic, salt, and black pepper, both inside the cavity and on the skin.
Place fresh herbs and lemon slices inside the cavity of each branzino.
Grease the grill grates with oil to prevent sticking.
Grill the branzino for about 4-5 minutes per side, or until the skin is crispy and the flesh is opaque and easily flakes with a fork.
Carefully flip the branzino using a wide spatula.
Grill the other side for an additional 4-5 minutes.
Once the fish is fully cooked, remove it from the grill.
Serve the grilled branzino hot, garnished with additional fresh herbs and lemon wedges on the side.
Optionally, drizzle with a bit of extra olive oil before serving.

Enjoy this simple and delicious grilled branzino, showcasing the natural flavors of the fish with a hint of garlic and lemon!

Anchovy and Garlic Butter Crostini

Ingredients:

- Baguette or French bread, sliced into 1/2-inch thick rounds
- 1/2 cup unsalted butter, softened
- 4-6 anchovy fillets, finely chopped
- 2 cloves garlic, minced
- 1 tablespoon fresh parsley, chopped (optional)
- Black pepper to taste

Instructions:

Preheat the oven to 375°F (190°C).
Arrange the bread slices on a baking sheet in a single layer.
Toast the bread in the preheated oven for about 8-10 minutes or until golden and crisp.
In a bowl, mix together the softened butter, finely chopped anchovy fillets, minced garlic, and chopped fresh parsley if using. You can use a fork or a small mixer to combine the ingredients.
Taste the anchovy and garlic butter and adjust the seasoning if needed. Keep in mind that anchovies are naturally salty.
Once the bread slices are toasted, spread a generous amount of the anchovy and garlic butter on each slice.
Place the buttered crostini back in the oven for an additional 5 minutes or until the butter is melted and bubbly.
Remove from the oven and sprinkle with a bit of black pepper.
Serve the Anchovy and Garlic Butter Crostini warm as an appetizer or snack.

Enjoy the savory and umami-packed flavors of anchovy and garlic on crispy crostini!

Beef Carpaccio

Ingredients:

- 8 ounces (about 225g) beef tenderloin or sirloin, very thinly sliced
- 2 cups arugula or mixed greens, for serving
- 1/4 cup extra-virgin olive oil
- 2 tablespoons lemon juice
- 1 teaspoon Dijon mustard
- 1 tablespoon capers, drained
- 1/4 cup shaved Parmesan cheese
- Salt and black pepper to taste
- Crusty bread or crostini, for serving

Instructions:

Place the thinly sliced beef on a serving platter or individual plates, arranging it in a single layer.
In a small bowl, whisk together the extra-virgin olive oil, lemon juice, Dijon mustard, salt, and black pepper to create the dressing.
Drizzle the dressing over the sliced beef.
Scatter the arugula or mixed greens over and around the beef.
Sprinkle capers evenly over the beef and greens.
Finish by shaving Parmesan cheese over the top.
Optionally, drizzle a bit more olive oil over the dish.
Serve the Beef Carpaccio immediately with crusty bread or crostini on the side.

Enjoy the delicate flavors of this classic Italian dish, where the thinly sliced beef is the star of the show, complemented by the freshness of the greens and the tangy dressing!

Spinach and Ricotta Stuffed Shells

Ingredients:

- 1 box (12 ounces) jumbo pasta shells
- 2 cups ricotta cheese
- 1 cup grated Parmesan cheese
- 1 large egg
- 2 cups fresh spinach, chopped
- 2 cloves garlic, minced
- 1 teaspoon dried oregano
- 1 teaspoon dried basil
- Salt and black pepper to taste
- 2 cups marinara sauce
- 1 1/2 cups shredded mozzarella cheese
- Fresh basil or parsley, chopped (for garnish)

Instructions:

Preheat the oven to 375°F (190°C).
Cook the jumbo pasta shells according to the package instructions. Drain and let them cool.
In a large mixing bowl, combine ricotta cheese, grated Parmesan cheese, egg, chopped fresh spinach, minced garlic, dried oregano, dried basil, salt, and black pepper. Mix well.
Spread a thin layer of marinara sauce in the bottom of a baking dish.
Stuff each cooked pasta shell with the ricotta and spinach mixture and place them in the baking dish.
Pour the remaining marinara sauce over the stuffed shells.
Sprinkle shredded mozzarella cheese evenly over the top.
Cover the baking dish with aluminum foil.
Bake in the preheated oven for 25-30 minutes, removing the foil for the last 10 minutes to allow the cheese to melt and brown slightly.
Once the cheese is bubbly and golden, remove the dish from the oven.
Garnish with chopped fresh basil or parsley.
Serve the Spinach and Ricotta Stuffed Shells hot, with additional marinara sauce if desired.

Enjoy this comforting and flavorful dish that combines the richness of ricotta and spinach with the classic taste of marinara sauce!

Limoncello Sorbet

Ingredients:

- 2 cups water
- 1 cup granulated sugar
- 1 cup fresh lemon juice (about 5-6 lemons)
- Zest of 2 lemons
- 1/2 cup Limoncello liqueur
- Lemon slices (for garnish)
- Mint leaves (for garnish)

Instructions:

In a saucepan, combine water and granulated sugar. Heat over medium heat, stirring occasionally, until the sugar completely dissolves. Remove from heat and let the syrup cool to room temperature.
In a large bowl, combine the fresh lemon juice and lemon zest.
Pour the cooled sugar syrup into the lemon mixture and stir to combine.
Add the Limoncello liqueur to the lemon mixture and mix well.
Transfer the mixture to an ice cream maker and churn according to the manufacturer's instructions until it reaches a slushy, frozen consistency.
If you don't have an ice cream maker, you can pour the mixture into a shallow, freezer-safe dish and freeze. Every 30 minutes, stir the mixture with a fork to break up ice crystals until it reaches the desired sorbet texture.
Once the Limoncello sorbet has the right consistency, transfer it to a lidded container and freeze for at least 4 hours or until firm.
Before serving, let the sorbet sit at room temperature for a few minutes to soften slightly.
Scoop the Limoncello Sorbet into bowls or cones.
Garnish with lemon slices and mint leaves.

Enjoy this refreshing and zesty Limoncello Sorbet as a delightful dessert or palate cleanser!

www.ingramcontent.com/pod-product-compliance
Lightning Source LLC
LaVergne TN
LVHW062048070526
838201LV00080B/2260